The Prayers
of
Jacob of Serugh

edited by

Mary Hansbury

SLG Press
Convent of the Incarnation Fairacres
Parker Street Oxford OX4 1TB England
www.slgpress.co.uk

First published by SLG Press 2015

ISBN 978-0-7283-0274-7 (paper)
ISBN 978-0-7283-0275-4 (ePub)
ISBN 978-0-7283-0276-1 (Kindle)
ISSN 0307-1405

Note on the cover illustration

The icon of Jacob of Serugh is based on an icon from St. Mark's Syriac Church in Jerusalem. The anonymous Syriac Life of Jacob suggested the elements of the inspiration of the Holy Spirit, which he received at any early age. The book in the hand of the angel indicates his prodigious literary achievements. His profound respect for the natural world, which he shared with St Ephrem the Syrian, is reflected in the trees growing around him.

Typeset by Oxford eBooks Ltd.
www.oxford-ebooks.com

I am giving the harp of my words to You
and let me borrow Your finger;
and in Your hymns let the sound whisper to Your glory.

On the Nativity, on page 30

Foreword

Among the Syriac Fathers, there are two outstanding poet saints, St Ephrem of Nisibis and St Jacob of Serugh, both from what is today southeast Turkey. Ephrem, who died in 373, the same year as St Athanasius, was exceptional in being a poet who was also a profound theologian, whereas Jacob excelled in his luminous insights into a large number of biblical passages, expressed in his delightful verse homilies. For Jacob (as indeed for both poets), the proper approach and interpretation of Scripture was closely connected with prayer, and so Jacob normally opens his homilies with a prayer-like invocation that he might be given inspiration as he sought to expound a particular passage. Many of these prefaces are beautiful little gems in their own right, and it is very good to have a selection of them provided here for a wider readership to enjoy.

Mary Hansbury, who is also an iconographer, has carried out wonderful work in making some of the riches of the little-known Syriac tradition available to an English-reading public through her translations. In an earlier publication, *On the Mother of God*, she provided translations of four of Jacob's verse homilies on Mary; these have been included in this book. Her other translations are of works by three great monastic authors, John the Solitary, Isaac of Nineveh and John of Dalyatha.

Sebastian Brock

Oxford, May 2015

Contents

INTRODUCTION

Jacob of Serugh was born in 451 in Curtam, a town on the Euphrates in Mesopotamia. His father was a priest of the village. He received his education at the School of Edessa and was there around 470, when the writings of Theodore of Mopsuestia would have been available in Syriac. However, he lived a quiet life of prayer and avoided the theological controversies following the Council of Chalcedon, which was held in the year he was born. His appointment as *Chorepiscopos* at Hawra is a clear sign of his talents in preaching and spiritual guidance. He served in this capacity until 518 when he was consecrated Bishop of Batnan, not far from Edessa, in the district of Serugh. Mar Jacob died 29 November 521. Both the Syrian Orthodox and Maronite Churches venerate him as a saint.

Jacob is one of the great poets of the early Syriac tradition. St Ephrem (d. 373), with the depth of his insights and his originality, can astound and even bewilder his readers, whereas Jacob is more straightforward—beautiful, but ever concerned about pastoral care and the edification of the Christian faithful. He developed this approach as he lived at a time of doctrinal conflict, which he chose to avoid. Rather, he focused on Scripture and the history of Salvation.

Divine love is central, and perhaps the most profound intuition of Jacob's work. The acts of divine mercy are the source of salvation, active in all phases of salvation history, and can only be understood in the context of Scripture. Jacob's affinity with, and affection for, Scripture remained so intense that he saw the depiction of the Son in every reading and every page of it. Perhaps this is what brought him to these beautiful prayers: in direct dialogue with Christ throughout the Scriptures. He uses them to describe the divine-human journey from the Tree of Knowledge to the Tree of Life, from the primordial Paradise to the eschatological Paradise. According to Jacob, when Adam attains this goal, he attains the full likeness of the Only-Begotten.

Jacob's thinking is essentially symbolic; like Ephrem's it shuns the logic and precision of Greek thought. Perhaps for this reason Jacob has been misunderstood and even considered as purely mythological. Fortunately, a re-evaluation in recent years has allowed his true thinking to emerge.[1] He understood the very structure of Christian life to be human praise uttered in response to divine life: 'The very pulse of my created being requires Your praise; and as by its nature, it hastens to give praise in Your presence' (p. 6).

These invocations of Jacob of Serugh are all superb examples of his soul at prayer before the mysteries of Salvation. They begin with 'O Exalted One'—his very first composition, according to the legendary life quoted here. In this selection from his many homilies, they end with a very moving comparison of the soul to a harp. One might compare them to the invocations which are embedded in the book of Psalms, so intense are they in their praise of God and intercession for all of humanity, the created world and the Church. These prayers exemplify the sacramental character of so much of Jacob's exegesis.

---

1 See the comments of A. Golitzin, 'The Image and Glory of God in Jacob of Se-rug's Homily, *On the Chariot that Ezekiel the Prophet Saw*,' St. Vladimir's Quarterly 47 (2003), 323-64, esp. 323-30. And see F. Rilliet, 'Une victime du tournant des études syriaques à la fin du XIXe siècle: retrospective sur Jacques de Saroug dans la science occidentale,' Aram 5 (1993), 465-80.

The Prayers
of
Jacob of Serugh

Life of Jacob of Serugh

Holy Mar Jacob, teacher, flute of the Holy Spirit and harp of the faithful church! He was from the village of Curtam which is near the Euphrates. He was born of the vows of faithful but barren parents. When he was three years old, he was presented in the Church by his mother on one of the festivals of Our Lord. At the time of the Liturgy, at the descent of the Holy Spirit on the Mysteries, the saint got down from the side of his mother and broke through the crowd and went to the altar and received three 'handfuls' of the Holy Spirit. From that time, he began to utter homilies and treatises. Immediately the bishops heard and they arose and came to him that they might examine him. They commanded him to recite a treatise concerning the chariot which Ezekiel had seen. So he began to recite: 'O Exalted One who sits on the heavenly chariot ...' Then they commanded that he deliver his teaching to the assembly in writing. And he began to set down homilies and treatises for the assembly when he was twenty-two years old. Afterwards he became bishop of the town of Serugh when he was sixty-seven and a half which was the year 830 of the Greeks, and 519 after the coming of Christ.

Then when he had filled the Church with the doctrine of salvation and had deluged the whole earth with his teaching and with his excellent interpretations, he departed to his Lord and was buried with honour in the town of Serugh in the year 833, on the 29th of November. All the years of his life were seventy: sixty-seven and a half before he became bishop and two and a half years while he was bishop.

On That Chariot Which Ezekiel the Prophet Saw

Exalted One, seated on the unsearchable chariot:
give me Your word, that on earth I may proclaim
    Your infinity.

Hidden One, exalted above the heavenly beings who
    bear You aloft,
grant that I may sing to You here in the regions below
    which You have redeemed.

Essence alone with knowledge of itself, how it exists,
speak distinctly in me that I may speak of You.

O! You, served by the legions of flame,
let my tongue serve You with the beauty of its singing.

Awesome One, by whom the sun is dazzled if it gazes
    upon You,
let my intellect gaze on You and be greatly moved to
    Your praise.

Hidden One, who are far from the assemblies of
    the sons of light,
reveal Your mysteries to me, that with its song my
    tongue may reveal You.

Borne by the cherubim, ineffable for us on earth,
speak through me for the sake of the mercies which
    You sustain.

Exalted One, who are far above the
    heavenly assemblies,
show me your wonder, that without prying I may
    speak of You.

Good Lord to whom dominions belong,
through You may I be stirred to speak of You.

O! You, blessed by the motion of the speaking wheels,
move my voice to multiply Your praise abundantly.

O! Power which carries its sign to the earth and yet
    remains far from it,
by that same Power which is from You, make this
    homily shine out to its listeners.

O! You who have spoken to us in part and through
    likenesses,[1]
let your instruction be voiced by me through the Son
    who is of Your essence.

O! hidden Word which came down to the
    earth openly,
give me of Your wealth, that I may impart it amongst
    the poor.

Lord most high, my mouth is insufficient for Your
    praise:
make a new mouth for me that it may proclaim
    Your songs.

On those chosen lips which You promised
    in the prophecy,[2]
may the wonderful teaching of Your divinity be voiced
    by me.

By the love which is the sum of all wisdom,
let my discourse extend to the telling of
    what is incomprehensible.

---

1 Cf. Heb. 1:1.
2 Zeph. 3:9.

By that faith which is the very breath of the new life,
may I reach out to Your recital, which is far above any
    who speak.

Through hope in You let me open my mouth to you,
    since I am convinced
that You will fill it with great praise as You
    have promised.

The open mouth as an adequate vessel—see!—is
    looking to You,
as You have promised: fill it with praise for Your love.

Were You to will it, it would be easy for the stones to
    speak to us of Your glory,
deign rather to be praised by lips that speak.

If the heights and depths were moved to speak,
the least would declare You in their orders.

May the silent ones not rise to Your praise instead
    of me,
let them rather move me to speak and wonder at
    Your doctrine.

If you had willed it so, the sea and the dry land would
    have sung Your praise.
Let the sea draw back and may the hymns of Your
    praise be sung by me.

If the earth should please You by speaking on
    Your behalf,
give it silence instead, O Giver, and to me Your praise.

Let these be at rest in their natures,
and may discourse on Your glory be richly
    pronounced by me.

Even if fallen from freedom, I am still Your image,
speak through Your image, which by Your gift was
    endowed with speech.

Let everything created abide in what is its own, as at
    its creation,
lest the order dear to Your working be perverted.

The sea for the fish, and the earth that it may bear the
    sons of men,
and the image with speech that it may be stirred all the
    day to Your praise.

By virtue of what is Yours, my Lord, limpid praise is
    offered You by those who speak,
what my nature has demanded of me is that I sing
    Your praise while I stand amazed.

The very pulse of my created being requires
    Your praise,
and, as by its nature, it hastens to You to give praise.

Your instruction has shone forth in me, though I did
    not insist on gathering
voices and words from the silent creatures.

It is from myself that both knowledge and wonder
    have come,[3]
and it is not from any other source that I have known
    what Your glory is.

---

3 Ps. 138:6.

It is from my creation, my Lord, that the knowledge of
  You comes that You are without limit,
and naturally I knew that I would find
  it incomprehensible.

You have concealed that knowledge, which knows
  Your business, in human nature,
and whoever knows not the error stays and is held fast
  by it.

Wherever should I go to seek You, my Judge, if I
  should go astray?
And to what place where You are not, if I
  should wander?

Were I to go up to the heavens – see! – You are there;
and if again I were to go down to Sheol, there, too,
  You are to be found.[4]

If my intellect were to lift me up to the heights, I
  would see You;
and if my understanding were to hurl me into the
  abyss, I would find You.

Heaven is too small and is filled by You, and You bear
  it up,
and the earth as well is inadequate and not sufficient
  for You, that
  You should be contained by it.

The world is too small for You, and all its regions do
  not suffice You,
and where would the intellect go looking were it to
  seek You out?

---

4 Ps. 139:8.

If I should go looking for You by casting my intellect
    beyond the world,
See! there You are, in the place void of
    other inhabitants.

If I should remain on this side of the world, You are
    not far away,
because You are close to whomever seeks to cleave
    to You.

If I should stand at the top of all the high places,
there are yet other heights there beneath you which
    are subject to You.

And if I descend beneath the bottom of all the depths,
beneath them all You stand, supporting the depths lest
    they grow weak.

You are resplendent in the height, and if You were to
    let go, it would not stand.
You hold fast the depth, and, once more, were You to
    abandon it, it would founder.

You embrace the air, and if You let go of it, it too
    would pass away.
The sea is grasped by You, and the fact that it will not
    become desolate is due to You.

The world is a great tent that You have pitched for all
    the species You have created,
and because of You it hangs established on nothing.

The heights are secured and the world built up,
    without foundations,
established without anything, it stands there as though
    on something.

Concerning the Blessed Virgin Mother of God, Mary

O Beneficent One, whose door is open to evil ones and
 to sinners,
grant me to enter and see Your beauty while I marvel.

O treasure of blessings, from which even the unjust
 are satiated,
may I be nourished by You because You are entirely
 life for him who partakes of You.

Cup which inebriates the soul with its draught, and it
 forgets its sufferings;
may I drink from You, become wise in You, and recite
 Your story.

O You, who grudgingly magnify our unworthy race,
 my word extols beautiful things with Your psalms.

Son of Greatness, who became a little child,
grant my feeble self to speak concerning
 Your greatness.

Son of the Most High, who wanted to be with
 earthly beings,
may my word be raised on high and speak to You.

You, our Lord, are an eloquent word which is full of
 life
and a great discourse which gives riches to the one
 who hears it.

Everyone who speaks about You is speaking because
 of You,
since You are word, rational mind and conscience.

Neither the thoughts of the soul stir without You,
nor do words move the lips except in You.

Lips give no sound without Your command,
nor is there hearing in the ear without Your favour.

Behold Your riches are lavished on those far and near;
Your door is opened for the good and the evil ones to
    come into You.

Everyone is rich in You, and You are enriching
    everyone without measure;
may my discourse be enriched by You with beauty
    and may it speak to You.

Son of the Virgin, grant me to speak about
    Your Mother,
while I acknowledge that the word concerning her is
    too exalted for us.

Concerning the Annunciation of the Mother of God

Son of God, who is the ineffable Word,
give me a word which sings Your praise abundantly.

O Hidden One who willed to be manifest, manifest
 Yourself to me
that I with a loud voice might bring to manifestation
 Your hidden story.

My mind is fertile, and it carries You on its thoughts;
with the mouth of the word, the voice brings You forth
 to the hearers.

However You have not just one birth, Son of God;
 but he
who is going to speak of Your birth should only speak
 of that other one.

The Father begot You beyond time, without a
 beginning
and again the Virgin Mother bore You
 without explanation.

Grant to my mouth that also it bear You with psalms,
since it is easy for You to come to birth because You
 are begotten.

The Father begot You and has granted that You
 become a child also for us,
for whatever belongs to the hidden Father, He has
 given to the world.

The Father in his love and by the grace which is in
    His nature,
sent this Son to us that in the end He might be Son also
    to us.

Concerning the Holy Mother of God, Mary,
When She Went to Elizabeth to See the Truth
Which Was Told to Her by Gabriel

Lord of all, let my harp be stirred by You for
    Your glory,
for because of You whoever is eager is able to speak
    to You.

My Lord, generate for me sounds and words,
    even music,
that my mouth may speak about You profusely.

My tongue will be Your pen, a scribe full of wisdom,
and with it will lovingly show forth Your discourse to
    be heard.

Let Your love stir me to speak to You with
    discernment
with an unworthy soul full of wonder concerning
    Your birth.

Son of the Most High who willed to be from mortals,
in You my poor word is raised up to Your Father's
    high place.

You are greater, my Lord, than reason and speech,
and small are the minds and the intellects to
    describe You.

The discourse about You is hidden from earthly beings
    and from heavenly ones;
Your tale is hidden from spiritual beings and from
    bodily creatures.

Neither men nor angels are sufficient for You,
because Your miracle is more sublime than earthly
    beings or heavenly ones.

If all the peoples would sing praise to You with their
    'Hosannas,'
yet the word about You would still be too exalted to be
    uttered by them.

A womb enclosed You, yet how can a word be
    sufficient for You?
A womb carried You, yet who does not fear to speak
    of You?

Arms carried You, but for someone to speak of You
    is audacious;
 breasts have nourished You, yet not to marvel at You
    is an ingratitude.

Heaven stood in awe, it diminished, it wasted away
    from Your greatness,
but a womb received, held and carried Your glory.

Because of these things, the learned one stumbles
    when he beholds You;
the word of the wise one is defeated, since it does not
    suffice for You.

Whenever the mind beheld that heaven is full of
    Your greatness,
it saw Your Shekinah dwelling in the womb; it
    is troubled.

On this account the disputant stumbles without
    knowing You;
his word is entangled in strife without praising You.

In faith, without stumbling because of Your lowliness,
grant me to receive You in my thoughts with wonder.

Even the sky is small for You, my Lord, if You will it,
but the womb of Mary is big for You because You
    so willed.

Because You so willed, a womb has contained You;
    unless You so willed,
all the ages would not suffice You, Son of the Lord of
    the universe.

Because it pleased You to dwell in the womb, in spite
    of Your greatness,
on this account, You are a marvel to the one who
    knows You.

Even when the womb of Mary bore You, because it
    pleased You,
all the ages were filled with You, because such
    You are.

Even if there was no place within the ends of the earth
    that was not filled with You,
You were dwelling in a span of flesh because You
    so willed.

For a great place, indeed, was not sufficient to
    contain You,
nor are You straitened by a little place if You
    stay there.

Heaven is small but the maiden is great according to
    Your will,
for that one is inadequate but this one is fruitful
    because You strengthened her.

On the Perpetual Virginity of Mary

Son of the Virgin, whose homily is too exalted for the
   wise ones,
fill me with Your gift, may I be illumined and may I
   speak of Your nativity.

Hidden One, who is distant and entirely concealed
   from the disputants,
reveal Yourself to me and may I speak of You
   without disputation.

Son of the Majesty, who willed to become small,
magnify my words with songs that I may recite
   Your beauties.

Son of the Highest One, who among the controversies
   is ineffable,
give me Your love that by it I may sing to You
   without controversy.

O Great One, who willed that the small womb might
   become His dwelling,
be pleased that with words, I may recite Your
   story lovingly.

The Father gave You freely to the world because of
   His love,[5]
   in that love, cast Your gift upon the needy ones.

With great price Your love ransomed us from
   the captors,
on account of us, then, freely You gave Your mercy to
   the whole world.

---

5 Cf. John 3:16.

You poured Your precious blood for me and with it
    You redeemed me,
possess me since You have purchased me, and
    enable me to possess Your word that I may recite
    Your story.

I am ransomed with a price bought and You my Lord
    were freely sold,
what does the world have to give and then to
    buy You?

What would Your hidden Father have received for
    His Beloved,
if He had given You with a great price on account
    of us?

It is pleasing to Him that He gave You freely
    to mankind,
since if You had to be bought for a great price, no one
    would have bought You.

Who would have had something to give as Your price,
    Son of God,
or what was there to him who would buy You to be
    exchanged for it?

Or what did Your own Father receive so that He
    gave You,
because all the worlds and their inhabitants are not
    worthy of You.

Since He saw that no one could give Your price and
    take You,
He gave You freely so that all might be rich in You.

Concerning the Burial, That Is to Say,
the Death of the Holy Virgin Mother of God, Mary
and How She Was Buried by the Apostles

Son, who in Your love inclined heaven and descended
　　to earth;
and put on a body and became man from the daughter
　　of David!

Mystical Offspring from whom the heights and the
　　depths are filled,
fill me with Your mystical instruction which brought
　　about two worlds.

Only-begotten Son, who fashioned man from nothing,
restore the discourse in my weary mind that I may
　　sing to You.

Son, who firmly fixed ten mortal senses in the
　　mortal body,
stay my thoughts and bring them to the place of
　　Your Father.

Christ, who have given the Spirit of life to man whom
　　You created,
pour into me Your living discernment, filled
　　with wonder.

Hidden-One, who are concealed even from the
　　Watchers and they do not see You,
shine upon me in stillness so that I may proclaim
　　openly about Your Mother.

O You, who healed the unclean man who had been
    brought near to You,
restore and heal the body and the soul of those who
    await You.

Light of Christ, which illumines the eyes that
    are darkened,
let Your light shine forth on my frailty, and I will be
    enlightened by You.

Lover of mankind, who wanted to become human in
    the flesh,
and rested upon and dwelt within the pure mother,
    the daughter of lights.

O You who dwelt with her for nine months and came
    to birth,
may my mind produce gifts of praise at Your
    mystical nativity.

O You, who were cherished with lullabies by the
    pure Mother,
may my tongue pour forth all praise of
    Your sweetness.

Son, who have visited us and fulfilled the
    whole Economy,
grant me to speak of the burial of the faithful one.

Your Mother endured many sufferings for Your sake;
every grief encompassed You and brought You to rest
    within the tomb.

How much terror the Mother of mercy felt at
    Your burial,
when the guards at the sepulchre seized her lest she
    draw near to You.

She endured sufferings when she saw that You were
    hung on the cross,
that with a spear they had pierced Your side
    at Golgotha;

and when the Jews had sealed the sepulchre in which
    had been placed
Your living body which gives life and remits debts.

And to this Mother, who endured these things for You,
the end had come to depart to the world which is full
    of blessings.

The name of Christ the King who was crucified
    on Golgotha,
grants life and sheds forth mercy on the one who
    invokes Him,

and also on me a sinner who is not capable of
    praising her,
the Mother of mercy, who brought You forth in
    the flesh.

O Son of God, by her prayers make Your peace to
    dwell
in heaven, in the depths, and among all the counsels of
    her sons.

Make wars to cease, and remove trials and plagues;
bestow calm and tranquility on seafarers.

Heal the infirm, cure the sick, fill the hungry;
be a Father to orphans whom death has left destitute.

In Your pity, drive out devils who harass mankind,
and exalt your Church to the four quarters of the
    globe, that it may sing Your praise.

Watch over priests and purify ministers;
be a guardian of old age and youth.

O Bridegroom Christ, to You be praise from
    every mouth,
and on us be mercy at all times. Amen, Amen.

On the Nativity of Our Redeemer According to the Flesh

Your Nativity, O Son of God, is a wonder and my
    mouth is inadequate
to narrate Your great story with my enfeebled tongue.

Your revelation is exalted above all human mouths
    and how is it possible
that I who am feeble should narrate the story of
    Your nativity?

O Lord, the whole world is not able to narrate Your
    story
and how shall I, an unworthy one, hasten to narrate
    Your story?

Your Father alone knows how Your birth took place,
and being but dust, by what mouth shall
    [a human being] speak about You?

Veiled is that human revelation of Yours even from
    our Mother,
so who is there to deal with Your divine nativity?

There is no mouth that is able to exhaust the telling of
    You except that of Your Father;
how then and by what means shall my tongue reach
    out to Your hidden being?

Concealed is Your story even from the Watchers, and
    with what expression
shall I send You the gifts of my frail words?

The Cherubim, though servants, have never learned
    where Your abode is,
and to which place shall my mind proceed to speak
    about You?

Where shall I seek You because being not afar,
    nevertheless you are concealed?
But how shall I speak about You, the manifest
    Nativity, for Your story is hidden?

To which place shall my senses fly to capture You?
To which place shall I look and see You as You
    are invisible?

Whither shall the mind tread its way to seek You there,
and on which path should the word move to recite
    Your glories?

Where will You be found, upon the chariot or
    with Mary;[6]
with Your Father, or with Joseph in the land of Judea;[7]

in the bosom of Your Father or indeed in the bosom
    of Mary;
with the physical mother or on the throne of crystal?[8]

Can one find You on the fiery wings of dense feathers,[9]
or are You carried about in the arms of the
    young mother?

------

6 Ezek. 1:26.
7 Mark 2:1.
8 Ezek. 1:22; Rev. 4:6.
9 2 Sam. 22:11; Ps. 18:10.

Shall I see You on the backs of the Cherubim,[10]
or does Your majesty dwell upon the knees of the
    believing woman?[11]

Is Your brightness in the legions of sparkling rays
    of fire,
or are You girded around as a pauper in swaddling
    clothes in the manger?[12]

Did Your essence dwell where there is no breath for
    the Watchers,
or have You laid hold of the humble breasts, together
    with our humanity?

Among the swift movements of that chariot are You
    being kept hidden?
Or are the lullabies of the destitute woman dear
    to You?

Are You sanctified by the tongues of fire,
or are You embraced by the mouth of virginity?

Are You carried high above the eloquent wheels,[13]
or are You honored by the hands of that daughter
    of David?

Are the pure beams of flames yoked to Your honour,
or are You clinging to the bosom of the daughter of
    the poor?

---

10 Ezek. 1:1ff.
11 Luke 1:45.
12 Luke 2:7.
13 Ezek. 1:19ff.

Do You have Your kingdom in the hidden tabernacle
    higher than the principalities,
or in the cave folded over by rock does Your
    authority reside?

From the abode of the Seraphim, 'Holy, holy, holy' is
    offered to You by the chant,[14]
or is it perchance the milk from the Shepherds that is
    offered to You?

Here below, indeed, shall I search for You, above shall
    I gaze on You, or are You present to all?
Are You at Ephrathah, or in heaven, or in all confines
    of the world?

My Lord, I am inadequate because Your story is
    fearsome and I am feeble.
Your homily is rich and my tongue is poor and by
    what means shall I comprehend You?

Serene is the search for You, but my mind is agitated
    and how shall I be able for it?
Your honour is luminous, but my mind is dark, so
    how shall I see You?

Shall I choose silence? But it breeds harm, seeing that
    it belongs to inertia.
Shall I venture to speak? But there is fear there, which
    frightens me.

I am perplexed between the two and which shall I take
    hold of?
I am afraid to be silent and I fear to speak, so what
    shall I do?

---

14 Isa. 6:3.

I am giving the harp of my words to You and let me
    borrow Your finger;
and in Your hymns let the sound whisper to
    Your glory.

By the impulse of the Spirit let my mind bring forth
    the homily of Your praise,
for I am not capable of Your homily: please speak
    through me.

I am the flute, when Your word is breath and Your
    story is the voice.
Please take control of it, and by Your means may we
    sing to You using what is Your own.

Stir up my words and my tongue by Your power to
    speak of You
and by Your gift let me sing the story of Your nativity.

Since Your first birth is concealed even from
    the Watchers,
make me worthy to sing out concerning this latter one
    from the daughter of David.

To that first birth even the mind will not venture
    to approach,
but concerning this birth, it does not attempt to speak.

And that first birth is not to be spoken of even by the
    tongue of flame.
About this, the mouth strives to narrate, because this is
    the gift of race.

Regarding that birth which is from eternity, not even
the Seraphim are able to inquire,
but towards this present one even the shepherds
have approached.

About that first birth only the Father is aware of how
it was;
but regarding this birth, the creation resounds together
with everything in it.

That birth is remote from all ranks of the heavenly
beings
but this one is approached even by the Magi with their
offerings.[15]

The hidden birth is concealed because even to the
Cherubim His place is alien
but this one is made manifest by the compassion that
He poured upon earthly beings.

Yet this manifest birth of Yours is not at all revealed to
the investigators,
so how, therefore, is one able to speak about that
hidden birth?

Neither that birth from the Father nor that from Mary
is explained
because unique is Your nativity, hidden as well as
revealed and it is ineffable.

Unique is Your birth beyond times, remote is the
telling of it;
but this other one is within the seals of virginity.

---

15 Matt. 2:1,11.

Regarding the first birth, one is not even able to say
    how or when,
while even that latter one perplexes the scribes by
    its splendour.

I will stay away from that distant birth which should
    not be investigated,
and let me press on to that which is close at hand,
    which is ineffable.

Since I am not capable, let me not be found wanting
    while meditating on it;
since I am not adequate, let me not be blamed because
    I am praising.

My Lord, look upon my will, what it prepares
    regarding Your story,
so that without negligence let my tongue engage itself
    in Your praise.

If the crown of my homily is not beautiful, it is not on
    account of me,
because all the gems I have received from You I am
    setting in it.

And even the arrangement of words is not beautiful,
    it is Your gift;
for Your great story is not belittled by my
    inadequate mouth.

For, if someone with a stutter invokes the king with a
    confused diction,
the name of the kingship is not belittled by
    the stammering.

And if the account of the divinity is narrated
by the ignorant, the divinity is never belittled.

With this agreement, behold, I am drawing near, not
    to comprehend,
but to make manifest by my words all of my desire.

On this great day I have sung praise to Your divinity;
on Your great day may I see the mercy of
    Your divinity.

On this day, with inadequate words, behold, I have
    glorified You;
at Your great dawn make me worthy to sing at length.

On this feast I have given the gifts of my words to
    Your church,
in that eternal feast let me be a wedding-guest at Your
    marriage feast.

On this feast, glory be to Your Father and to
    You exaltation,
and the crown of victory to the Holy Spirit, and mercy
    be upon us.

On the Nativity of Our Lord

May my word be moved to speak about Your Nativity,
O Son of the Rich One who resembles His Father in
  His hiddenness.

About Your Nativity, may many things be spoken
  through me,
O true Son who is totally light to the One who
  loves Him.

Concerning that Being of Yours, no one is able
  to speak;
concerning what You have become, let me speak of
  You, Lord while I am wondering.

With respect to You, no one is able to speak, my Lord;
with respect to us, grant me that I may speak about
  You lovingly.

With regard to Your being God, the discourse about
  You is beyond the power of the speakers,
but because You are human, behold, we speak about
  You every day.

If You had not descended to our earth we would not
  have been able to speak about You,
for who is able to speak about You in Your place that
  is concealed from all?

About Your having come I am seeking, my Lord,
  to speak,
for Your compassion has made You subject to words
  on the road You have set.

I have not gazed above where fire dazzles forth
    from You;
in the depths I have seen You, and here in our place I
    am speaking about You.

Your love compelled You on account of us to come to
    our place.
About Your advent grant me a beautiful discourse.

Eyes have seen You and hands among the earthly
    beings have touched You,
and behold, the good and the bad speak about You
    with their tongues.

You descended from Your place and because You are
    mingled with the earthly beings,
the scribes saw You and everyone has composed a
    homily to offer You.

It has pleased You and You have come,
    the Ancient of Days, to become a babe,
and behold, the aged in the gatherings praise
    You abundantly.

It pleased Your Father that You should become a child,
    and on account of that,
children have yearned to sing many praises to You
    with their hosannas.[16]

A virgin has conceived You, and so let the company of
    virgins be aroused;
let them stir up praise with wonder to Your Father on
    account of You.

---

16 Matt. 21:15.

Arms embraced You and behold, the babes in arms
are sealed with Your name, and are clothed by
    You spiritually.

Your love appointed for You a new mother from
    among women
and the mothers thronged together with their
    husbands to give praise to Your name.

From Your Father the whole of Your story has come
    close to us,
and love has united You in lineage with us so that we
    might sing praises to You.

You became one of us and behold You are ours while
    You are our Lord,
and anyone who seeks to speak of Your story is
    entitled to do so.

Immanuel, behold, You are with us in our vicinity.[17]
Therefore, the tongues that were not worthy of You
    also spoke of You.

If your story had been kept in silence with
    Your Father,
behold, all would have been silent and the world
    would have been still, without Your praise.

And since Compassion sent You forth into the open
    and set You among the troublesome,
on account of You the earth is stirred up, has babbled,
    and clamoured.

---

17 Isa. 7:14.

One magnifies You while he does not add any
    greatness to You.
One belittles You but littleness is not to be found
    in You.

One speaks about You abundantly with love
and one is moved with wonder and was silenced by
    Your story.

One glorified himself to investigate Your birth, and
    became a mockery,
because he imagined that he knew, yet he was not
    aware that he did not know You.

There is the 'wise person' who became puffed up with
    book-learning
so as to speak of You, my Lord, but he was driven off
    because he assaulted You.

There is the 'ignorant' who while not knowing how
    to speak,
loves You and becomes greater than the 'wise' in all
    his way.

There is a 'knowledge' that has ascended to see how
    exalted You are,
but it burst, fell and destroyed itself in the
    great chasm.

Your way is exalted above doctrines and the learned,
and on account of this the scribes stumble against it
    when they investigate it.

Your economy is hidden in its story from
    human beings,
and on account of this when someone speaks of You
    he is troubled.

A womb has contained You, but how can the mouth
        contain You to speak of You,
the Word, which is even higher than the world, and it
    is inaudible.

Knees carried You, O Valiant One, the Bearer
        of creation,
and if someone speaks, he trembles, shakes, and
    becomes terrified.

On the bosom of Mary as an infant You
        were embraced,
and too small is the mouth for the word which
    narrates Your story.

A young girl gave You, the Sustainer, borrowed milk,
and with Your right hand that stretched out the
    heavens, You were grasping the breast.

Arms have carried You, while that chariot of the
    Cherubim[18] was shaken as a result of You, as it stirs
    up Your praise with blessings.

Everything of Yours when spoken of is exalted,
beyond what is customary and what belongs to nature,
    so who is   capable of understanding You?

---

18 Ezek. 1:4ff.

Let the virgin Church who is betrothed to You rejoice
    in You, my Lord,
when she sings to You new praise with an
    exalted voice.

Let the gatherings of the peoples and congregations
    rejoice in You
and the tongue too, which though unworthy, sang
    Your praise.

Let the speaker and also the hearers rejoice in You,
    my Lord,
because by Your Nativity You have gladdened them,
    to You be glory!

*On the Presentation of Our Lord in the Temple
and on the Reception of Him by Simeon*

O Most Ancient of all, who became a new born babe in
    the blessed woman,
open my lips to sing praises of Your birth.

O 'Fashioner of Babes' whose love compelled Him to
    become a new born babe,
fashion in me the word that is full of your
    amazing grace.

O Son of the virgin who was not known carnally by
    any mortals,
instruct my tongue to be an advocate of Your songs.

O the One, hidden from the Watchers, who became
    man in the body with which He clothed himself,
grant me grace that I may diligently become a hireling
    of Your story.

O Marvel who cannot be spoken of by human beings,
bestow on me Your love that I may sing praises to You
    without prying.

O Church, praise with your beautiful songs
the 'Aged Child' who by His birth gave freedom
    to you.

O Christ, who came and proclaimed liberation to those
    who were bound prisoners,
let loose from Your Church the grievous knots
    of strife.[19]

---

19 Luke 10:24; Matt. 13:17.

O Son of God, who gladdened Simeon by His birth, make us all rejoice in the good hope of faith in You.

On the Baptism of Our Redeemer in the Jordan

'The waters have truly seen You, God, and they feared:
also the abysses trembled, and the clouds of the air
    sprinkled water.[20]

All the nature of the waters perceived that You have
    visited them:
seas, abysses, rivers, springs and pools.

They pressed hard together to be blessed by
    Your footsteps,
because Your great manifestation that came upon
    them caused them to tremble.

You stepped upon the Jordan as upon the summit of
    all seas;
and the extremities of the abysses and of the floods
    trembled at Your power.

The whole nature of the waters was stirred by
    Your descent,
because by Your baptism You made everyone worthy
    of pardon.

The waters of seas, although distant, are not distant
because the power of Your holiness has stirred
    mystically and visited them.

For this reason the waters truly saw You and
    they feared.[21]
Even the abysses trembled because by Your descent
    You have caused them to tremble.

---

20 Ps. 77:16-17.
21 Ps. 77:16.

Clouds sprinkled water into the river when You
    were baptized,
so that they too should not be deprived of
    Your descent.

Behold, even the heights of heaven proclaimed again
    through Your heavenly Father,
so that in His testimony the earth should perceive that
    You are the Only-Begotten.

Your lightning illumined the earth and it saw the
    glorious Light.
The earth was troubled by darkness until You came.

Waters saw You and they feared You as the Lord.
The breath of Your energy heated them while You
    were descending.'

O Perfect One, who came so that He might perfect the
    insufficient by the waters;
let Your great mercy overflow from You upon
    my insufficiency.

Blessed is He who came and was baptized by His
    envoy as it pleased Him.
He is the one who sanctified baptism; to Him be glory.

*On the Transfiguration of the Figure of Our Lord on the
Mountain of Tabor
and on Moses and Elijah Who Were Talking with Him*

Behold, the impulse of Your homily urges me, O Son
    of God.
Speak it through me abundantly in hymns of wonder.

Your story stirred within me to move itself towards
    the hearers.
Give power to my word to demonstrate the beauty of
    the countenance of the Light.

Behold, my thoughts surge greatly at Your glory.
Let them vanish into You and from You may they bear
    fruit as discourses of praise.

The mind marvelled about You, let the mouth speak
    about You, though You are incomprehensible.
The mind gazed on You, so that the discourse might
    depict how beautiful You are.

Pour mercy upon my lips enabling them to speak
    about You,
and let my tongue put on the Spirit and let it sing
    about Your majesty.

I would speak about You, my Lord, not that I will
    comprehend You, because You are infinite,
but let me speak about You, how exalted You are
    above the preachers.

The mouth and the ear shall be bedewed by You but
    you remain as You are,
and while I am speaking of You, remain with me, for
    You are ineffable.

Within the bounds of utterance let the homily depict
  You while I am speaking,
but once I have spoken, You are beyond it and
  within it.

My Lord, let the exaltedness of Your story descend to
  me, until I encounter it;
and when I have cleaved to it, let it rise up to its
  summit and take its position.

Either descend, O my Lord, to my word and let it
  speak about You,
or raise it up that it may reach out towards you and
  sing to You.

Lower Yourself to the homily so that it may speak
  about You on account of Your love,
and let the word be exalted with You on account of
  You until it has spoken of You.

It is easy for You to become small and it is easy for
  You to exalt the one who adheres to You;
by adherence to Your homily, let my word be exalted,
  O Son of the Lord of all.

You, my Lord have both greatness as well
  as smallness,
because You are both God and man and the whole of
  You is with everyone.[22]

With Your Father, on account of Him, You are
  like Him,
and with us, on account of us, again You are like us.

---

22 1 Cor. 9:22.

On account of Your Father You are like Your Father in
    Your glory,
and on account of us You became like us to become
    one of us.

Exalted is Your revelation, glorious is the discourse
    concerning You and beautiful is Your story;
even if all mouths should speak of Your glory they are
    not adequate before You.

On the Sunday of the Hosannas

O Fountain of Life from which the dead drank and
    became alive,[23]
pour Yourself into me and quench my thirst from
    Your fountain.[24]

O Drink that flowed into the thirsty earth and it
    produced fruit;
let me drink from You and I shall call out openly how
    sweet You are.

O New Well which they have hewn out with the lance
    upon Golgotha,
rise up and give me the drink for my mind which is in
    need of Your fountain.[25]

O Son of God who called himself 'Living Water',[26]
give me to drink and when I shall be satiated by You,
    let me speak about You.

O Fountain which from the beginning descended from
    the height to the earth;
with Your drink let my mind bring forth fruits of
    praise to Your Father.

Grant me grace to speak about You, not that
    I would comprehend You because You
    are incomprehensible;
but let me preach to those who hear me because You
    are unattainable.

---

23 Ps. 6:9.
24 Rev. 21:6.
25 John 19:34.
26 John 4:10,11; 7:38.

For who, without love, can attain to You so as to speak
   of You, O Lord, as You are,
since this story is superior to the understanding of
   human beings?

As far as love's extent, it will speak about
   Your revelation;
give me a word which narrates the splendour of
   your humility.

From the chariot to the borrowed colt, young-one of
   an ass,[27]
Your love made You descend, but who is capable of
   narrating Your story?[28]

From that impenetrable legion of the Cherubim,[29]
the humble conveyance carried You in solemn
   procession into our country and how did it
   suffice You?

From the place of the wheels, and the Presence and
   wings of flame
mercy carried You and behold, a young one of an ass
   carries You in solemn procession.[30]

From that majesty of the throne that is full of light,[31]
to the littleness whose love is sincere with the children.

From that summit full of revolving eyes,[32]
You have come to this most despicable conveyance in
   the world.

---

27 Dan. 7:9.
28 Matt. 21: 5, John 12: 15.
29 Ezek. 10:1-22.
30 Ezek. 1:16-20; Exod. 25:30.
31 Isa. 6:1ff.
32 Ezek. 1:18.

From among the heavenly orders and choirs which
    exist out of the flame
to the small gathering that carries the branches in the
    streets of Zion.[33]

Now how shall one speak who speaks of Your story,
and in which place shall the mouth tell about You if it
    tells about You?

Behold in the chariot your brightness blinds the
    heavenly beings
but feeble and ugly is the colt that carried You among
    earthly beings.

You are blessed by the moving of the eloquent wheels,
and You are glorified by the branches of the palm-trees
    in the gatherings.

You are above and beneath, in majesty and
    in feebleness;
on high and in the depth below, who is able to speak
    about You?

On account of us, Immanuel, You are like us.
And with Your Father, because of Him, You are
    like Him.

Behold the fiery Cherubim bless You with their
    hovering
and also the children glorify You with their Hosannas.

Behold, all regions solemnly escort You in their
    own ways,
the height with its light and the depth with the
    branches that are from its trees.

---

33 Luke 19:28-40.

Above He is mighty, held in awe by the flame
below on earth He is humble, clothed with
    all poverty.

O my Lord, the mouths of human beings praise You
    with their tongues,
and the dumb natures in their own ways sing
    Your praise.

O my Lord, the whole of nature gives thanks to you
    because it has been renewed by You,
for the whole of it ought to acknowledge with wonder
    Your humility.

Heaven worships You because you humbled Yourself
    towards earthly beings
and the earth praises You because You are higher than
    the heavenly beings.

The redeemed gathering of the Church of the Peoples
    shouts joyfully to You, my Lord;
because You liberated her from the stumbling-blocks
    of vain idols.

The daughter of the Arameans exults on Your day and
    is glad with You;
instead the daughter of Hebrews became sad, treated
    You with contempt and was angry.

Behold, the young people praise You with the
    branches of the trees
and the voice of praise of the aged is mixed with that
    of the children.

Behold the shepherds and their flocks adore You
instead of that flock that crucified its Shepherd
    on Golgotha.

Behold, the gatherings of the Peoples in all places bless
    You
instead of the fact that You were reviled by that band
    of Caiaphas.

Behold, they call out to You, 'Holy, holy, holy', in the
    assemblies
instead of the gathering of the People that had called
    out, 'He is guilty of death.'

Behold, all voices from all mouths are singing Your
    praise
with all tongues, since you have stirred them up for
    Your praise.

Fiery Seraphim with awesome chanting of, 'Holy,
    holy, holy',
while being covered with your flame, stir up
    Your praise.

Glorious Cherubim who are bound to You by
    the flame,
with great impulses bless Your awesome Person daily.

Many thousands of heavenly beings sing Your glory
without ceasing from the praise of their sanctification.

Behold, the virgin Church, whom You brought back
    from the captors,
resounds in You, she is enriched in You, and rejoices
    in You;

all are giving thanks to You because by Your coming
  everything is renewed;
You are blessed by all, to You praise from all tongues.

On the Great Sunday of the Resurrection

On the great day of Yours, in which the whole
    creation rejoices,
allow me to speak abundantly about
    Your resurrection.

On the feast that gladdened both the angels and
    the disciples,
make me also joyful by Your gift to sing about You.

O Valiant One who ascended in brilliance from within
    the tomb;
let me speak about You, concerning Your victory filled
    with wonder.

On Your great feast heaven is glad and earth exults
because in You heaven and earth, that were at enmity,
    were reconciled.

On the Resurrection of Our Lord

The resurrection of the Son is again stirred up that it
    might be spoken by me.
Again, my Lord, give me the voice that attains to the
    preaching of You.

O Great Sea, pour out into me the homily of Your
    kindness
and give me the word that I may proclaim Your
    story prudently.

You skilfully conquered the region of death when it
    had confined You
because through weakness You uprooted Sheol which
    was closed up.

From the place of sufferings Your voice looked forth
    in a mighty way,
and caused alarm to the powers of darkness that
    were flourishing.

On Your great day gladden Your Church, O Son of
    God
and sign her children who are placed in you
    possession with the Cross of Light.

May peace reign among the ranks of the priests.
May her feasts multiply in Your noble slaying which is
    observed by her.

May the pastors and their chief pastors be reconciled
    in her,
and let the staff of Your Cross be a guard to
    their flocks.

May the wolves that attempt her destruction be
   choked by her,
and by Your crucifixion may she drive them away
   from her sheepfolds.

May the Church be secure from disputes of wicked
   laborers
and may it work daily with the master-builders of
   the faith.

May Your feast be a day which removes
   all controversies;
and from this time onward may peace reign in
   Your assemblies.

Let the quarrel of the shepherds come to an end so that
   they may not be in turmoil,
and may only the rational sheep dwell in
   fertile meadows.

You are the one Shepherd; may there be one group as
   shepherds in You
and from the single stream of Your side may all sheep
   be given to drink.[34]

Keep her chief-pastors lest they would be divided
   against their brethren.
But in Your love may they tend Your flocks diligently.

May Your feast open the door to peace so that peace
   may control the earth
and curb from the earth quarrels of kings and rulers.

---

34 John 19:34.

May Your day be a shield that keeps away all evils,
and by it, may the orderings of the world be kept
    from chastisement.

May Your resurrection bring peace to Your Church
    from Your Father
and may great peace rise before her and may she be
    sheltered in it.

Keep in harmony the shepherds and their chief
    shepherds
and equally the innocent flocks with their assemblies.

Keep Your covenant from the perversion that
    surrounds it;
and may the choirs in the assemblies stand firm
    in splendour.

May the great path of communion rejoice on Your day,
since You are guarding peace for men with
    their wives.

May the mothers together with their offspring be glad
    in You
and to the barren ones grant the petitions of
    their supplications.

Support the aged and give education to the infants.
Have pity on sinners and for the righteous keep the
    deposit of faith.

Pour out Your gift upon the rich and the poor,
full is Your treasure house, grant the petitions of
    all ranks.

On Your great day, grant the petitioners their requests.
Blessed is Your resurrection which has made the
gloomy earth joyful.

On the Ascension of Our Lord to Heaven

My Lord, let me not be silent from Your praise, not
    even when I am dead,
for anyone who lives in You, on account of You, shall
    not die.[35]

Watchful is Your Word and the silence of Sheol will
    not make it sleep:
let Your Word be spoken through me so that the
    coming generations shall speak it.

Exalted is Your Word even beyond death, wherever
    it be,
because it is alive with You and the depths of Sheol do
    not confine it.

Your Word, O Lord, is not confined, subject
    to destruction,
for it resembles You because regions do not
    confine You.

You remained upon the throne but the womb of Mary
    was filled by You.
In heaven is Your dwelling but on earth is Your birth.[36]

A womb contained You, a manger carried You, knees
    lifted You up;
heaven is Your throne; a cave Your bridal chamber, the
    earth Your span.

The sea is the hollow of Your hand, the firmament
    Your sign, O Son of God!
Your power is everywhere but Your glory is wrapped
    in swaddling clothes!

35 John 5:24.
36 Ezek. 1:26; Isa. 6:1.

Heaven is small, a virgin carries and gives You milk.
The Seraph is veiled, but Joseph is unveiled and
embraces You.[37]

You are hidden together with Your Father but You are
revealed on account of us.
For the Watchers there is Your fire, but for humanity
Your humility.

The sound of Your blessings is in the motion of the
eloquent wheels
and the sound of Your lullabies is from the lips of a
solitary woman.[38]

Clouds are Your sign, and for Your mouth are drops
of milk;
on a bosom You are carried and upon the chariot You
are carried about.

Above is the Mighty One at whom the armies of
angels tremble,
below is the Humble One mingled with the poor
every day.

In heaven awesome, on the earth beloved, and who is
equal to You?
You are hidden as well as revealed; how can anyone
be competent to speak of You?

The eloquent were in an uproar, the Scribes disputed
over You; 'the wise' were defeated;
the fishermen conquered and the untaught became
brilliant in Your proclamation.

---

37 Isa. 6:2ff.
38 Ezek. 1:15ff.

You are the Son of God, You are the Son of Man and
    You are the Son of Mary.
You are the Son of the Most High and among the
    beings below You are incomprehensible.

You came from the height, shone out from the depth,
    You came from the Father.
You acquired for Yourself a mother, You became a
    babe, and who can investigate You?

Hidden is Your fire, revealed is Your appearance,
    exalted is Your revelation.
Let mouths tremble and not dare to investigate You.

The mouth is abundantly empowered for the praise
    of You;
and it is not easy to search into You, as You are, the
    Son of the Lord of all.

*On the Holy Sunday of Pentecost
and on the Division of the Tongues
and on the Gifts of the Apostles*

O Lord, kindly open to me the door of Your treasury,
so that I may carry along and bring forth all kinds
  of advantages.

Grant me the word that by which I may recite
  Your grandeur,
and an exalted voice that proclaims about Your glory
  all the day.

Let a homily of wonder be impelled within me by
  Your gift;
and in the hearers, wonder and love regarding
  Your story.

O Lord, through Your Word let my word run between
  the verses
to gather from Your reading all sorts of advantages
  for us.

Breathe into me Your Spirit and let me pronounce
  gently the praises of Your hymns;
grant me the word and I shall be an advocate of
  Your truths.

You who confused all tongues in the land of Babel,[39]
give me a single tongue of truth with which I may
  sing to You.

O Instructor, who supplies his tribe with all wisdom,
may I become wise in You to narrate Your wonders.

---

39 Gen. 11:7.

O Hidden Teacher, from whom all
    instructions proceed,
fill me with Your instruction, I shall distribute every
    day from Your treasures.

By the punishment of those who rebelled, one can
    learn of You,
how the whole of You is mercy to the one who hastens
    to take refuge in You.

On Tamar and on the Symbol of the Church

Come to me, Lord, and bring the mercy of
    Your kindness;
sprinkle it on my strings, and let them extol You with
    their songs.
Come, my Lord and my God, and blow in me as into
    an empty reed
so that I may give forth sounds with a stirring of love,
    without confusion.
Come, O Lord and grant me fair utterance that is filled
    with beauty
so that I may speak thereby, as I worship in
    great wonder.
Come, You who are not distant in giving each day all
    kinds of good things
to the person who seeks to receive freely the wealth
    that comes from You.
You are close by, O Son of God, You are close at hand
to grant each day all kinds of requests for those
    who ask.
You are close by, and here You are, with us
    Emmanuel:
You have wearied Yourself by bringing blessings and
    riches for the entire world.
You were with us, and like us too, for all our sakes,
and now heights and depths worship you in
    their domains.
The height sent You, and the depth received You in
    great wonder,
and look, height and depth are filled by You, for You
    are boundless.

You came to the world—and the heights were not
  emptied of You,
You resided in the Virgin – and the heaven remained
  full of Your glory.
All the heights, in their domains, are not sufficient
  for You,
and see how all the depths, and those who dwell in
  them hold You in honour.
You came from the Father, You shone out from a
  mother, You became an infant.

Mercy mingled You with humanity, so that You might
  save it.
You scattered Your treasures over the poor and made
  them rich,
the dead came to life in You, and the world, that had
  become corrupted, was set in order.
You became the Daytime, and the whole earth became
  light from You:
night fled away, for all creation had been submerged
  in it.
You came down like rain upon the lands that
  lay waste,
You made them like Paradise full of blessings.
You shone out as the Sun of righteousness over the
  entire earth,
and Your dawn dissipated the darkness from
  every region.
You are the Bread of Life, for the dead consumed You
  and were resurrected in You.
You are the good wine, for by You all who mourn
  are comforted.

With oil, You consigned to oblivion the wickedness of
    Adam who had been smitten;
You applied wine to his wounds, seeing that he had
    been wounded;
with living water you cleansed away his filth, for he
    had become sullied,
and he was renewed in You, and returned to Eden
    which he had lost.
O Son of God, exalted in Your highway and full
    of blessings,
set out upon it are the milestones of peace for him who
    travels on it.
You, Lord, are the Light; You are Life, Lord; You are
    the Resurrection.
You are the great Treasure Store by whose treasures
    the poor have become rich.
When Your compassionate Father fashioned Adam in
    His image
it was You He depicted in him, for in You the dust that
    had multiplied would be adorned.
He gave to Adam Your likeness when He created him,
    so that he might put it on[40]
and by it reign over all created things and
    acquire them.
With a breath of life did Christ make him when he
    made him,
so that he might keep His place in the world until He
    would come.
You were hidden in Your Father, and He revealed You
    in Adam when He created Him:
He depicted in him the likeness of Your bodily
    existence and Your revelation.

---

40 Gen. 1:26-27.

The depiction of the King travelled down all
    the generations,
transmitted mysteriously over the lineages.
So that God Himself might be mingled
    amongst humanity,
He gave His image from the very beginning of
    Creation so that human   beings might be made
    in it,
for He was preparing to send His Son, the Only-
    Begotten;
and in this same fashion he came into the open, in
    bodily form:
for in the likeness of the Only-Begotten of the
    Godhead
He depicted Adam when He fashioned him, in a
    great mystery.
He then came back and took the likeness of His
    servant from within the womb,
and became like it while He was delivering it from
    the Rebel.
He came to His nativity, He took up His likeness, He
    delivered His image.
He commenced and He completed in accordance with
    His will in great love.

On the Red Heifer
The blood of Christ is like strong wine, showing its strength in the capacity to understand symbols.

1. Behold, I approach the treasury of Your symbols to
   acquire wealth;
grant me an abundance from the wealth of
   Your crucifixion,

2. so that my mind conceives the passion of Your
   death, O Son of God.
By the birth pangs of your killing may it deliver a
   homily about things that are true.

3. Your blood ferments within me; let me mix the wine
   of Your sacrificial death.
Draw out within me, and I will give thirsty nations
   drink from Your fountain,

4. Your wine, new and divine: mix without sparing.
so that when they preserve it and are preserved by it,
   they are entrusted to Your care.

5. Grant me speech not that I may put an end to
   Your hiddeness,
but that, though amazed, I may speak what may not
   be apprehended.

6. Your waves of Your utterances have knocked me
   over; I swim in the midst of Your floods.
Lord of the seas, give me Your hand; let me be
   dragged out by You.

7. Your symbols surround me, like legions of all kind
   of strong warriors;
each one pulls me that it might speak to me about the
   things that reveal You.

8. I see that the wealth of Your symbols is stored up in
   the pathway of books,
and to me fell the labour that I should bear off some of
   it, and become rich by it.

9. Study has called me to the banquet of Your
   great death,
and mixed blood for me, and it seethes up to display
   its strength.

… the Kingdom of Heaven is like unto Leaven …

O Leaven of Life who was sent to us from the
    Most High,
knead Yourself into me so that I may acquire the taste
    of Your gentleness;
O Son of God who has been mingled with us,
    becoming one of us,
May I become one with You, and may my tongue tell
    of You;
O Great One who has descended right down to the
    extremity of littleness,
may Your utterance grow in me, for I, with the
    iniquity of my hands, am so little.
O Lord of the heights who willed to lower Yourself to
    the very depth,
grant to me, who am in the depth, utterance that will
    attain to the height of Your true place.
O Living Fire who cast Your fire into all the world,[41]
may the fire that cleanses away all sins flare up in me;
with Your fire which scours away iniquity refine me
    and make me pure,
lest I burn in that fire at the End Time that so
    terrifies me.
You came to cast fire into the world and it has fallen
upon those who listen to Your word, which itself
    is fire;
Your fire has caught alight in me as well: may I be
    fervent in speaking;
blow upon me so that I may burn brightly as a result
    of You, as I address You.
May the mind be stirred by the fire of Your love, and
    may it bear fruit in telling of You,

---

41 Luke 12:49; Cf. Mal. 3:2.

for wherever this fire falls, it effects peace in
     its gentleness.
The whole world is full of the undergrowth of denial,
but fire has fallen upon it and devoured the thorns,
     and the earth is restored;
the tangle of iniquity came about through the entire
     world's sin,
but the Crucified One has cultivated it, and see how
     good seeds are sprouting there!
With the nails and the lance He has cleared it,
     liberating it from the tares,
removing from it all plants that are bitter;
He has opened up all the remote rocky places,
and now the entire earth bears crops of praise,
For uprooted from it are all bad plants with their wild
     growth and thorns,
while the cypress and sweet-scented myrtle exult![42]

---

42 Cf. Isa. 55:13.

On the Sinful Woman

Lord, I long for Your forgiveness to come to me.
Give to me tears so that I may ask for mercy while
    there is an opportunity.

I thirst for mercy and without it I cannot exist.
Sea of Mercy, pour out on me the streams of
    Your kindness.

The confused sins of an evil world are traps to me;
by Your mercy, Lord, destroy them, and I will
    be delivered.

Like a legion of demons thirsting for blood, my sins
    have surrounded me.
Come, Mighty Warrior, to the aid of a humble worker.

The King of Error has poured down his arrows aiming
    at my death.
Commander, apply to me Your remedy by which I
    may be healed.

Your treasury is not too little to give mercy to those
    who do not deserve it:
because You even loved the prostitute dearly, when
    she approached You.

For none but crushed people seek Your remedy;
and he who does not even need it, mercy is not dear
    to him.

The good physician, however, is not glorified but
    by ulcers.
For what does he add to a sound body if it comes close
    to him?

It is in wounds that he shows the power of his skill.
He rightly takes his fee and glory according to his
    healing power.

The physician shines in the stricken ones when they
    are healed.
And Your great compassion shines out in sinners
    when they are absolved.

Because You have mercy, I acquired sins, and thus I
    expect
that whenever You pardon me, Your compassion will
    shine in me.

I do not say that my transgression is too great
    to pardon,
because Your compassion is greater than the sea:
    purify me in it!

I prepared the work for Your mercy every day when I
    was a sinner,
so You should not be idle from forgiveness, because it
    is lovely to You.

For the physician wishes that the ulcers might increase
    in his vicinity,
so that he might acquire from them both profits
    and praises.

Here are some wounds: bring Your medication so that
    it might shine in me,
because it is very beautiful to You when You heal the
    stricken ones.

On the Ten Virgins

O heavenly Bridegroom who has called all the ages to
    Your marriage feast,
shine upon me and I will give light and will speak of
    You profusely.
O Son of the Kingdom who has summoned the ages to
    the banquet hall,
may Your glory stir me to sound forth Your story.
May Your Word be a path for me, my Lord, and I will
    walk in it,
and may Your homily be full of light, that I may see
    Your truth in Your Psalms.
I am Your flute, blow upon me and I will sing
    beautifully:
distinct sounds of praise with the stirrings of the soul.
Without breath there is no sound from those
    who speak,
by means of Your breath may my voice be with those
    who listen.

Wherever there is a voice, breath is what sustains it,
moving it perceptively to be heard.
May Your grace, my Lord, be the life-giving breath,
that by its movement, stirs up in me hymns
    of instruction.
I will speak about You and You will speak in me about
    Your coming,
for You are the Word, in You all words are spoken.
You are the image of the Father's Glory
and in You one sees clearly all the beauty of the ages.
You are the reflection of the Godhead which is
    all light,[43]

---

43 Cf. Heb. 1:3.

and Your appearing enlightens the soul in secret as it
    narrates Your story.

Stir up in me, my Lord, both word and voice for the
    listeners
that I might wondrously proclaim Your riches among
    the discerning.
Speak clearly to me, my Lord of Your coming
while prudently I marvel at Your great manifestation.
For a soul which is full of faith, it is easy to hearken to
    that manifestation with great wonder.

Behold, in the Scriptures the revelation of the Son
    is depicted,
and whoever searches them, the eye of his soul will
    see it.
From the divine readings, one recognizes
what the Kingdom will be when it is revealed.
The luminous Son showed us when He was teaching
how He will come and what He will be like when He
    appears to us.
Before He comes, He has foreshadowed how He
    will come,
and how the generations will go out to meet Him in
    that great day.
He depicted that day and His Kingdom, when it will
    be revealed,
as a glorious bridegroom and fair virgins.[44]

---

44 Matt. 25:1-12.

On the Name Emmanuel

With mercy look upon me, O Son of God, who are like
    unto Your Father,
that I might praise You in simplicity without
    questioning!

I am a ten-stringed harp which You have fashioned:
pluck me that I may play for Your glory, yes on
    account of You!

Strum me with Your finger and move my
    silent strings,
that sweet song may be uttered by me with a
    resounding voice.

For a string cannot produce a sound without
    being struck,
nor does a mouth have speech without Your gift.

A harp cannot give melody of its own accord,
and unless its player plucks it, it remains mute
    and silent.

The harpist strums skillfully with his finger
and awakens a sound in strings that lie silent.

Play me, O my Master, for You hold me and I behold
    You:
inspire in me rich praise concerning Your
    manifestation!

Even if a sound is given to a silent string, it is not
    its own,
but it looks for a skillful blow to awaken sound in it.

The string is my soul, and behold, it is silent without
    Your glorification!
Pluck it, that You might play my sounds of praise in a
    wondrous manner!

You have no need of the glorification of earthly beings,
but so as to be exalted the human race has great need
    of You.

For Your Father sent You forth to exalt the sons
    of men,
to raise them from the dung-hill where they were
    laid low.

Mercy united You with the sons of men who were lost,
and by Your commingling You found them so as to
    bring them back again.

You were of us, and behold, You were with us in our
    very neighbourhood:
You are Emmanuel who comes to free the
    Father's servants.

O beloved Son, behold, You are with us and are our
    God!
For indeed You are called Emmanuel by the prophecy.

Notes

1. page 1: *Life of Jacob of Serugh:* This anonymous Syriac Life of Jacob of Serugh is preserved in MS Vat Syr 37, 16r., and published by J. S. Assemani, *Bibliotheca Orientalis*, I, 286-289.

2. page 3: *On That Chariot…* A. Golitzin (tr.), *Homiliae selectae Mar Jacobi Sarugensis*, ed. Paul Bedjan (Paris,1908), Homily 125, Vol. IV, 543-547.

3. page 9: *Concerning the Blessed Virgin Mother of God…* M. Hansbury (tr.), *On the Mother of God* (New York, Crestwood: St. Vladimir's Seminary, 1998), 17-18.

4. page 11: *Concerning the Annunciation…* Ibid. 43.

5. page 13: *Concerning … Mary When She went to Elizabeth…* Ibid. 65-67.

6. page 16: *On the Perpetual Virginity of Mary:* James Puthuparampil, *Mariological Thought of Mar Jacob of Serugh (451-521)*, Moran 'Etho 25 (Kottayam, 2005), Appendix, i-ii.

7. page 18: *Concerning the Burial … of the Holy Virgin…* M. Hansbury, op. cit. 89-90.

8. page 22: *On the Nativity of Our Redeemer…* Thomas Kollamparampil (tr.), *Jacob of Serugh, Select Festal Homilies*, (Bangalore: Dharmaram Publications,

1997), 'On the Nativity of Our Redeemer (I),' 41: lines 1-103; 1139-1146.

9. page 30: *On the Nativity of Our Lord*: Ibid., 'On the Nativity of Our Lord (III),' 110: lines 1-70; 364-371.

10. page 36: *On the Presentation of Our Lord...* Ibid., 'On the Presentation of Our Lord, 141: lines 1-12; 389-392.

11. page 38: *On the Baptism of Our Redeemer...* Ibid., 'On the Baptism of Our Redeemer,' 162: lines 420-439; 529-532.

12. page 40: *On the Transfiguration...* Ibid., 'On the Transfiguration,' 204: lines 1-32.

13. page 43: *On the Sunday of the Hosannas:* Ibid., 'On the Sunday of Hosannas,' 247: lines 1-44; 275-304.

14. page 49: *On the Great Sunday of the Resurrection:* Ibid., 'On the Great Sunday of the Resurrection,' 293: lines 1-8.

15. page 50: *On the Resurrection of Our Lord...* Ibid., 'On the Resurrection of Our Lord,' 307: lines 1-8; 201-238.

16. page 54: *On the Ascension...* Ibid., 'On the Ascension of Our Lord to Heaven,' 331: lines 11-46.

17. page 57: *On the Holy Sunday of Pentecost...* Ibid.,

'On the Holy Sunday of Pentecost,' 354: lines 1-18.

18. page 59: *On Tamar…* S. Brock (tr.), 'Jacob of Serugh's Verse Homily on Tamar (Gen. 38),' *Le Muséon* 115:3-4 (2002), 293-94.

19. page 63: *On the Red Heifer:* D. Lane (tr.), 'Jacob of Sarug: *On the Red Heifer,' The Harp* XV (2002), 25-42.

20. page 65: *On the Leaven…* S. Brock (tr.), Homily 86, Bedjan, Vol. III, 411.

21. page 67: *On the Sinful Woman:* S. Johnson (tr.), 'The Sinful Woman: a Memra by Jacob of Serugh,' *Sobornost* 24:1 (2002), 57-58.

22. page 69: *On the Ten Virgins*: M. Hansbury (tr.), Homily 50, Bedjan, Vol. II ,168.

23. page 71: *On the Name Emmanuel:* D. Miller (tr.), Homily 40, Bedjan, Vol. II, 160.

Further Reading

Thomas Kollamparampil, *Salvation in Christ according to Jacob of Serugh* (Piscataway NJ: Gorgias Press, 2010).

James Puthuparampil, *Mariological Thought of Mar Jacob of Serugh (451-521)* Moran 'Etho 25 (Kottayam, 2005).